EXPLORING & CUSTOMIZING SIDE NOTES

Blue - exploring sidenotes lead to the pages with additional information.
Green - customizing sidenotes lead to the pages with customizable content.

PICK & APPLY

pages with illustrations are easily numbered

theory pages are mainly located with odd numbers

VIOLET BOOKMARKS
(main themes)

MAIN THEMES &
CUSTOMIZING PAGES

VISUAL MEMORY MATRIX
(last page with images)

how to use it

5

LEARN TO PLAY BETTER

1. when you play **WELL**, you feel **POSITIVE**
2. when you are not playing well, you are not feeling good
3. usually when you are not feeling good, you probably are not going to play well
4. you can learn to change your thinking into **POSITIVE THOUGHTS** and that will allow you to **PLAY BETTER**

Welcome! Your time has come!

Welcome to the pocket guide **POCKET TENNIS PSYCHOLOGY**™. You made a decision to become a better tennis player. This book is designed to help you rise in the mental game of tennis. Come and discover the uniqueness in yourself as a player! **I.A.M. Tennis - Instant Anger Management in Tennis** is unique system which supports your abilities and takes your game to the next level. You will learn how to control your emotions and have advantage ahead of the competition. I.A.M Tennis means that you can use it immediately, whenever you need. **Customize your game & determine your results** by controlling internal balance in an easy and incredibly efficient way. **Advanced mental coaching** is specially crafted to be fitted for your skills. It is you who determines your game, your effort, your way, your results. It is you who has control over your freedom. All you have to do is put this book into your pocket and

enjoy the next best shot!

Before reading and applying hints from the guide - POCKET TENNIS PSYCHOLOGY™, the reader should consider every implication for his / her physical and mental health. Author of this pocket guide does not take any responsibility over actions of individuals that use hints without any reasonable consideration. Every progress in improving mental abilities relies on regular practice with a certified tennis instructor.

Performance Pocket Guide - POCKET TENNIS PSYCHOLOGY™ is based on training - Advanced Mental Coaching created by Mario Beky.

Published in 2018 by Mgr. Mario Beky.
Hrádza 83, Michalová 976 57, Slovakia
mail@mariobeky.com
Number of publication 19
Number of edition 1
Printed by Mgr. Mario Beky
Grammar correction Jacqueline Kisova.
Made in Slovakia. UV-1P-OW2MC
All rights reserved.
Copyright © Mgr. Mario Beky
Graphic design © Mgr. Mario Beky
Print - ISBN 978-80-570-4179-5
EAN 9788057041795

HOW TO USE THIS GUIDE?

READ IT & USE IT!

We recommend reading the whole publication before putting it in the action. This pocket guide is easy to understand and if you know how to use it, it can save you plenty of time.

The pocket guide - Pocket Tennis Psychology provides multilevel user availability for the easiest possible utilization. It's divided into theory, graphics & customizable content (starting on page **58**). Save precious time and find as fast as possible the best solution with advanced searching.

ACCESSIBILITY

This pocket guide offers you several ways how to quickly find useful info anytime you need.

1. Main themes (page **78**)
2. Advanced bookmarking system (**ABS**)
3. Exploring & Customizing Sidenotes (**EX&CS**)
4. List of key phrases (page **77**)
5. Court map indicators (page **76**)
6. Visual memory matrix (**last page - 80**)

You are unique in many ways, so are your searching preferences. Use the one which suits you best.

ABS - ADVANCED BOOKMARKING SYSTEM

advantage

main themes text
in current color code

Outer coloring of the bookmark refers to the color code of pages
gray - generic
blue - exploring
green - customizing

IMMEDIATE RESPONSE

- **immediate response** - active feedback to the new and challenging situation (unexpected, unwanted, difficult) with less rehearsal time and less possibilities to handle it with proper re-action

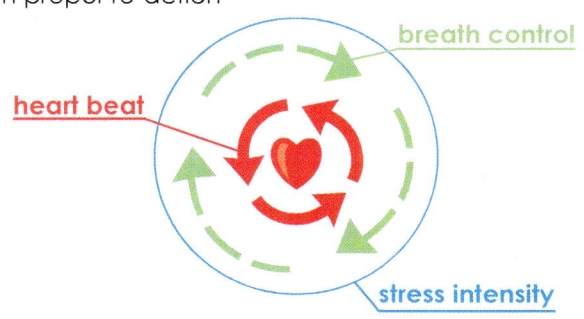

STEP BY STEP BUILD THE FORTRESS OF HEALTHY CONFIDENCE

- try to immediately control the stress reaction with slowing down the process of stress & reversing it
- in real game (especially in competition) will come up situations that will have the instant impact upon the player
- the more pleasant or difficult situation the more uncontrollable emotional reaction it creates
- the key of handling those types of situations is to be prepared in advance
  1. practice with a golf PRO (to be technically in top shape)
  2. practice the multiple relaxation techniques

immediate response

psychology & tennis

PSYCHOLOGY & TENNIS
PRESSURE & PERFORMANCE

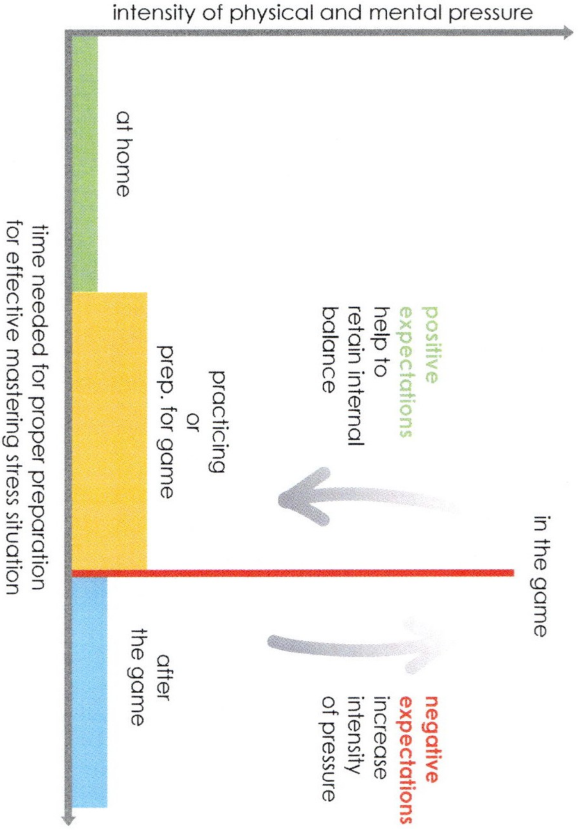

intensity of physical and mental pressure

at home

practicing or prep. for game

in the game

after the game

positive expectations help to retain internal balance

negative expectations increase intensity of pressure

time needed for proper preparation for effective mastering stress situation

UNDERSTAND YOUR MIND!
LEARNING TO USE PSYCHOLOGY AS A MENTAL ADVANTAGE!

- using **psychology** means to:
  - identify
  - describe
  - control
    - your **behavior** (and that means):
      - what do you feel
      - how do you act

- always go to the shot or putt with **ONE positive thought**
- always end the shot or putt with **ONE positive thought**
- your thoughts are what is leading your hands and body
- success has 3 pillars – ambition, technique, etiquette
- make sure you are supporting all of them equally

- when you will **learn to strengthen** your **ability to handle stress**, you will need to use less time and energy to be calmed down and return to your state of well-being
- the more you will evaluate the situation with negative expectations, the longer time will be needed for the mental processing ➡ the more unprepared you will be when you'll face the next shot

BEING PREPARED means **BEING ONE STEP AHEAD**

psychology & tennis

tennis & stress

**THINK AND PLAY
THE EASY WAY**

UNDERSTAND THE ORIGIN OF STRESS & CONTROL IT!

4 anti-stress preparation guidelines:

1st - off court preparation
- auto-regulation, auto-suggestion of positive thoughts

2nd - during practicing
- confrontation with the tennis court environment

3rd - short time between shots on the tennis court
- active relaxing techniques

4th - after the game
- you are full of fresh experience, review it!

- if you are **shaking, sweating** and your **heartrate has risen,** you are probably facing a situation which your mind(consciously or unconsciously) defined as potentially dangerous
- **stress reactions** are inherited to **protect us** from dangerous situations
- you cannot avoid them but after reasoning, your body can be calmed down - **LEARN TO CONTROL IT**

WHEN A **SITUATION** CREATES A **REACTION**, EXPLORE THE **REALITY**, TRY TO **REASON** AND **RELEASE THE PRESSURE**

1. **SITUATION**
   - on your way home through a dark street suddenly something BIG and DARK comes out from the shadows (situation thoughts - **you are going to play against a strong opponent** or **facing a player with strong shots who is also very fast on the court**)

2. **REACTION**
   - your hands, legs and whole body starts to shake and your heartbeat goes to 180 bpm in 2 seconds; warmth has prepared the body for RUN or FIGHT (reaction thoughts - **possible humiliation with shots missing the playing area or miss-hitting shots**)

3. **REALITY**
   - the BIG person is heading towards you, his face is now illuminated with street light and you are recognizing your father (reality thoughts - **your opponent already missed few shots in a row**)

4. **REASONING / RELEASING PRESSURE**
   - (reasoning thoughts - **the game goes on & you start to realize that this player isn't as good as you thought him to be. You're playing well today. You can win it!**)

**SOMETIMES BAD SHOTS HAPPEN TO EVERY PLAYER
YOU CAN SAVE THE WHOLE PROCESS
WITH JUST ONE POSITIVE THOUGHT**
(AND WITHOUT ANY NEGATIVE THOUGHT!)

tennis & stress

REVERSE PROCESS OF STRESS

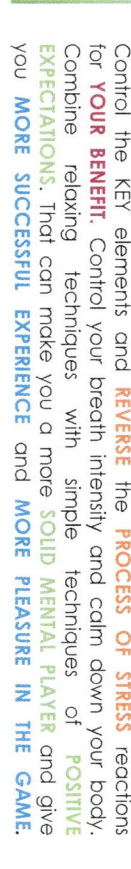

When you're unexpectedly facing the unknown situation your internal security system is getting activated. Breath intensity increases, which rises your heart beat, your muscles start to shake, body warms up rapidly to prepare you for the RUN or FIGHT. Unfortunately that can affect your shots in a bad way.

Control the KEY elements and **REVERSE** the **PROCESS OF STRESS** reactions for **YOUR BENEFIT**. Control your breath intensity and calm down your body. Combine relaxing techniques with simple techniques of **POSITIVE EXPECTATIONS**. That can make you a more **SOLID MENTAL PLAYER** and give you **MORE SUCCESSFUL EXPERIENCE** and **MORE PLEASURE IN THE GAME.**

TIME ISSUE MANAGEMENT

- every match has time for the way it should be played, don't waste your **time & energy!**
- in a moment you are losing time, **your opponents** are gaining time
- with more time, they gain **more self-confidence**, which helps them to be **more successful** - that means you are less successful
- if your opponents are losing time, **you are gaining** it, you are getting more confidence which will help you to be become more successful
- always **think forward with positive expectations**
- you cannot turn back time if hitting an unwanted shot
- all energy taken from an ACTUAL NEGATIVE EVALUATION means saving more energy into the **NEXT POSITIVE APPROACH** from the following shot

OTHER ISSUES MANAGEMENT

- **stress** roots from **many origins** - partner, parents, coach
- motivate yourself to **prepare your mind for a challenge**
- start with acceptance **"I accept to play my best!"**
- it is not what my partner, sponsor, fans want, it is what

I AM PRIVILEGED TO ACQUIRE

- have at least 1 person who gives you **POSITIVE SUPPORT**
- there is never an external factor which influences you, it is always **YOUR THOUGHTS**

tennis & stress

tennis & stress

CLEARING THE VISUALIZATION -
orienting on achieving goals

my **GOALS**
- **my** decision
- **my** effort
- **my** expectations
- **my** shot
- **my** responsibility

external stirs

- sponsor
- opponents
- partner
- club members
- friends
- coach
- family
- fans

shell

THE THICKER **MIND SHELL** YOU'LL LEARN TO CREATE IN THE **CRITICAL MOMENT OF THE SHOT** THE LESS YOU'LL BE AFFECTED BY EXTERNAL STIRS ON THE WAY TO **ACHIEVING YOUR GOALS**

THE ACTUAL SHOT IS
THE
MOST IMPORTANT
SHOT OF YOUR LIFE

HOW TO MANAGE YOUR THOUGHTS?
ALLOW YOURSELF TO FOCUS ON ACTUAL MOMENT (SWING) &
YOUR HANDS, YOUR THOUGHTS, YOUR GAME
WILL BE REWARDED

- focus on actual moment – THIS MOMENT
- you live in **this moment**, you are not living yesterday, not tomorrow, not in 10 minutes, you are living **NOW**
- **YOUR ball, YOUR shot, YOUR trophy** is waiting for you
- it wasn't here yesterday, it won't be here tomorrow
- bomb yourself with **POSITIVE** thoughts & **ENERGY** and **RELAX**!
- if you are confused about your **emotions**, make them **numbers**
  - **– 10 is top negative, 0 is neutral, +10 is top positive**
- some people may push you, don't forget that it is YOUR EFFORT, YOUR EXPECTATIONS, YOUR GAME

tennis & stress

relaxing techniques

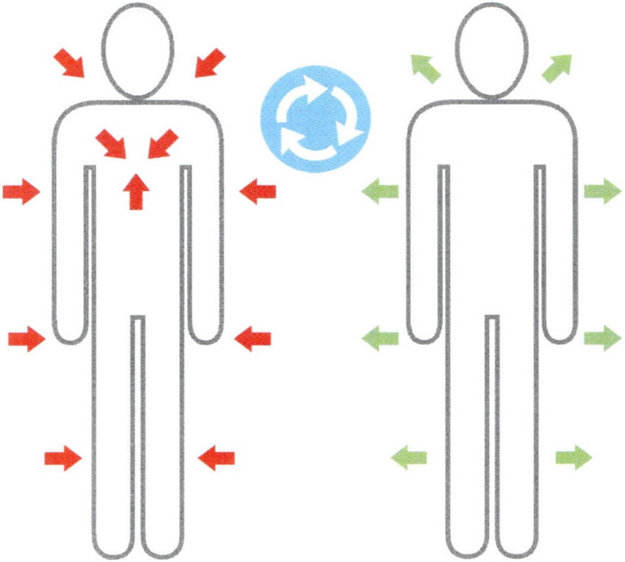

RELAXING TECHNIQUES

RELAXING BEFORE PRACTICING

- you can do it on the couch or in the car seat
1. **apply** medium **pressure** on muscles of your whole body or just one part of your body for **2 seconds**
2. **release** the pressure for **2 seconds**
3. **repeat** each session but **not more than 3 times consecutive** (with every new session increase time by 2, by 4, by 6 sec.)

RELAXING BEFORE PRACTICING

- practicing is a KNOWN situation
- you know what to expect, therefore you can be **better prepared**
- **mental relax = physical relax**
- renew, restart positive memory

- use **autosugestive thoughts** (goals) which should be

> **POSITIVE, SPECIFIC & ACHIEVABLE:**
>
> - **I CAN** do it!
> - Today is **MY DAY!**
> - Today I will play a **GREAT MATCH!**
> - I have **PRACTICED VERY HARD** for this!
> - I will play shots **LIKE NEVER BEFORE!**

- avoid NEGATIVE THOUGHTS or thoughts with any negative content like:

- I will not fail.
- There will be no bogeys on my scorecard.
- I did not practice much, hopefully it won't harm my game.
- I cannot lose any stroke.
- I hope I will not make many mistakes.

relaxing techniques

relaxing techniques

TUNNEL OF ATTENTION

Consistency is more than power!

BALANCE YOURSELF!

Watch your grip!

Rhythm is Monte-Carlo!

I didn't put wristband in my bag!

FLY! GET OFF MY NOSE!

I should practice more!

Just don't hit into the alleys!!!

- 1st memory sector
- 2nd memory sector
- out of attention

time continuity

RELAXING BEFORE THE GAME

- **prepare** yourself **in long term** especially when you are thinking about your professional career in tennis
- consult your health with professionals
- leave yourself a time reserve before the match
- make a **list of things** that you will carry **in a bag** when practicing and when going into competition

RELAXING AFTER THE SWING

- **your result is determined** - how you think 3 to 5 seconds before shooting and up to 20 seconds after shooting
- you have **enough time to think** about the shot but never enough time to spare on other issues
- you have to practice your **internal playing autopilot** - every thought which is needed to make the shot must be set free therefore **execute** everything learned **without thinking** about it

The tunnel of attention

- create your own circle of thoughts - our thoughts go in circles - **FIRST info IN, FIRST info OUT -** (1st thought of series of thoughts which enters the attention is the one which is also first forgotten)
- you probably know it from your personal experience when you are repeating phrases in time of leaving home or office "I must have - phone, keys, glasses... phone, keys, glasses..."

relaxing techniques

 **relaxing techniques**

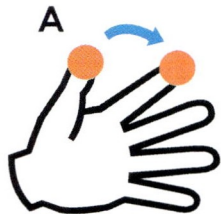

1. inhale approx. 30% of your lung capacity for 2 seconds
2. use connection between thumb and index finger as reference point A

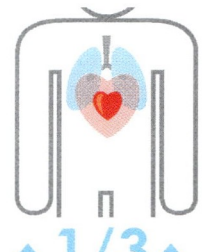

↑ **1/3** ↑

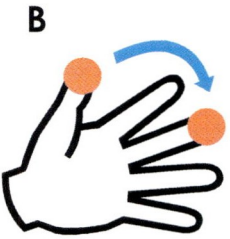

3. inhale approx. 60% of your lung capacity for 2 seconds
4. use connection between thumb and middle finger as reference point B

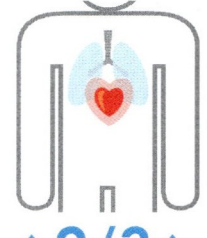

↑ **2/3** ↑

5. inhale full capacity of your lungs for 2 seconds
6. use connection between thumb and ring finger as reference point C

↑ **3/3** ↑

Use this exercise in situations in which you need to calm down quickly without necessary attention.

RELAXING AFTER THE SHOT

- **your next step will depend:**
    50% - on how you encountered the shot
    50% - on your playing attitude
- if you are losing control over your emotions, remember to return to the basic theory of stress (10)
- otherwise adrenaline level can ruin your final score
- always do:
    - **realistic reasoning**
    - **positive oriented evaluation**
- manually lower the intensity of pressure, stress (read more instructions on page above) (20)
- breath intensity control – reverse process of stress (12)

I DON'T WANT TO RUN AWAY,
I WANT TO FACE IT,
I WANT TO UNDERSTAND IT,
I WANT TO CONTROL IT,
I WANT TO WIN!

If you want to learn more about staying calm under pressure and achieving the best personal performance, join the **Ultimate Mental Game Training** in **Mario Beky Academy**

relaxing techniques

rethinking

RETHINKING THE MENTAL APPROACH

5:5 < 6:0 > 0:5

tie 5:5 isn't better than win 6:0, but is better than 0:5

40:40ᴬ < 40:0 > 0:40

beginning of the match
0:0

ending of the match
0:6 0:5

opponents advantage isn't better than yours, but is better than you being close to losing the entire set

30:0 < 40:0 > 15:0

The more advantage you gain the more you'll be hungry to get the entire dominance over your opponent. Every stagnation in your approach is giving more space for opponent's attack. In tennis your primary objective is to gain dominance over your opponent by getting the control over your emotions.

2 RULES OF TRIVIAL DOMINATION

1. **every better score is better than any bad score**
2. **every initial neutral or negative beginning is better than the final negative result**

RETHINKING THE MENTAL APPROACH

- if you are not satisfied with actual results it is time for **REASONING AND REVIEWING** MISTAKES & FAULTS
- **YOU HAVE TO PRACTICE WITH a professional tennis coach** at least once a month
- the tennis PRO is looking at you from the other side
- if you feel confident on the practicing court but you don't **deliver scores in tournaments** maybe you should consider playing at least 1 risky shot per set
- when playing a tournament, **reconsider,**
  sometimes the GAIN is worth of the RISK
- **play a LOT to learn** to recognize **DECIDING MOMENTS**

RETHINK THE MENTAL APPROACH & DO THE MATH
every time you are feeling pressured
and you don't know how to continue

- the difference between the next worse score are always 2 points, 2 REASONS how NOT TO RUIN the whole score chart (with making bad shot increases probability of hitting the next bad shot multiple times)
- BUT! if you are not The Swiss Maestro and the tournament you are actually playing is not the US OPEN, try to change your thinking **from RISKY to REASONABLE**
- your game is highly specific, therefore IF your rackets are custom fitted for your body & game level, why don't you **fit your mental game to play your best?**

rethinking

cognitions

COGNITIONS & THE TENNIS GAME

Some serving positions do offer more control over opponent's movement on the court than the others.

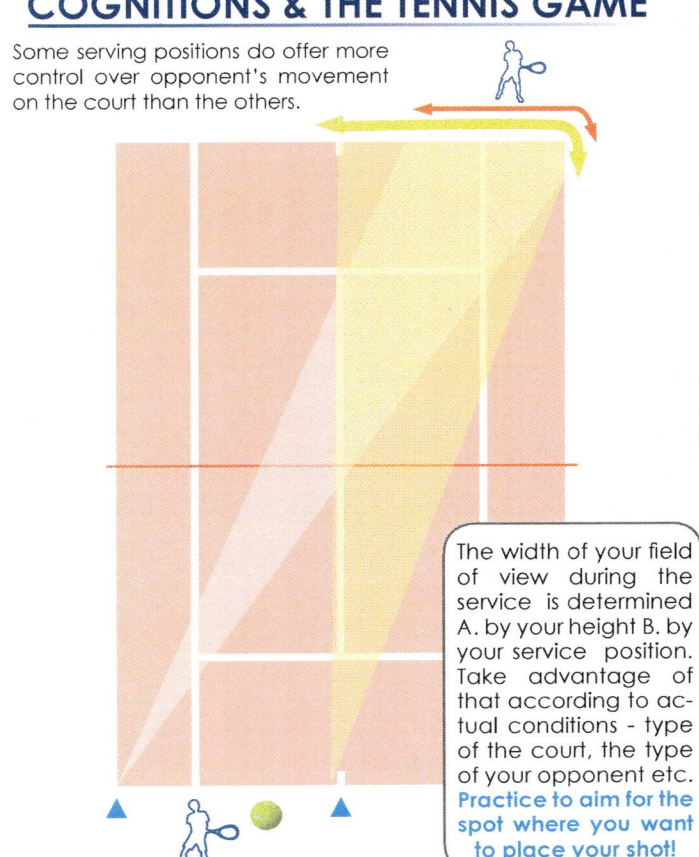

The width of your field of view during the service is determined A. by your height B. by your service position. Take advantage of that according to actual conditions - type of the court, the type of your opponent etc. **Practice to aim for the spot where you want to place your shot!**

- **cognitions** are processes by which the sensory input is transformed into your mind
- cognitions help you **transform** all received **data into language** that your **mind will understand**
- recognizing processes would start over and over again, therefore our mind uses stored data which is similar to what we see, sense, feel and experience - these data are sometimes called **anchors**
- anchors **help** our brain to **categorize** and compare **similar information**

  for example – we look at a map of Italy as a boot
- **knowledge is golden**, being prepared = to know
  - know yourself - know your playing style, body+mind capabilities, strengths, weaknesses, limits, equipment
  - know match conditions court, ball, general/local rules, tournament schedule, time zone, weather
  - know your opponent - playing style, coach, body capabilities, strengths, weaknesses, limits, equipment
  - know your weaknesses - to recognize when your opponent is trying to attack on them & stop him!
  - practice to resist the attack on your weakness
  - (lick the lip) - never let your opponent to recognize fully that you're attacking his weakness because he will try to block your attack
  - use everything legal for getting more options in the game itself before you will enter the match

JUST PLAYING WITHOUT REHEARSAL IS PURE GAMBLING

cognitions

THREE PILLARS OF SUCCESS

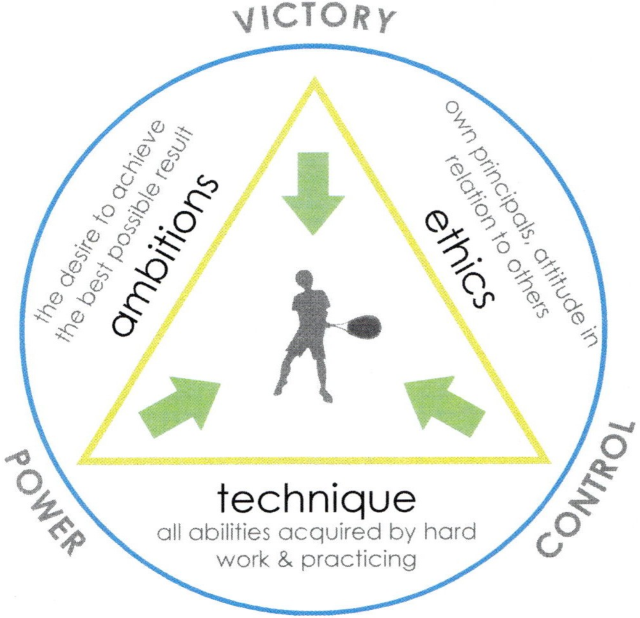

VICTORY

the desire to achieve the best possible result

ambitions

own principals, attitude in relation to others

ethics

technique
all abilities acquired by hard work & practicing

POWER **CONTROL**

YOU ARE THE PLAYER IN THE MIDDLE OF THE TRIANGLE AND IF YOU WANT TO BE SUCCESSFUL, YOU NEED TO WORK ON THESE THREE PILLARS EVENLY OTHERWISE YOU WILL LOSE THE BALANCE

CLEAR VISION

- to not be affected by **external stirs**, you have to **clear your visualization - "remove the stirs"**
  - if your co-player, coach, partner, tennis court, country, sponsor are origins that affect your game in a negative way, change them
- ignoring external stirs is never an easy process, because we are sensitive beings
- you need plenty of

PATIENCE AND SPECIFIC GOAL

healthy game confidence - specifics:

- **summarize your goals** and set yourself a goal before you are going to practice, or play a round
- when you don't pick a goal, you don't have direction where you want to go - you're either A. moving forward or B. you're moving backward
- make sure your goals are **semi difficult**
- watch all three pillars of success closely:
  - ethics
  - ambitions
  - technique of the game

POWER + CONTROL = VICTORY

- make sure that you work on every one of them with the same amount of energy and attention
- if one of 3 pillars fades, you will lose balance and fail

cognitions

advanced practicing

ADVANCED PRACTICING TECHNIQUES

INTENSIVE - ALL AROUND LEVEL

- perfecting the all-around playing capabilities can boost your **game - self confidence**
- **practice with professional tennis coach** at least once a month all **basic fundamentals** over and over again
- practice for "two marathons" instead of one - this will give you **advantage over the others** in the real game
- always practice to adjust to **actual circumstances** of actual match and the opponent you're facing
- define what you can and can't control:
  - **your behavior**
  - **behavior of your opponent**
  - **type of the tennis court**
  - **type of the tennis ball**
  - **the weather, time, crowd, etc.**
- accept the fact – it is less possible to achieve a **perfect result in everything**, you can just **get close**
- work hard on **the 2 most important tennis statistics** –
  - **WIN vs. LOSS**
  - **PROGRESS vs. REGRESS**

PLAYING CONDITIONS #1

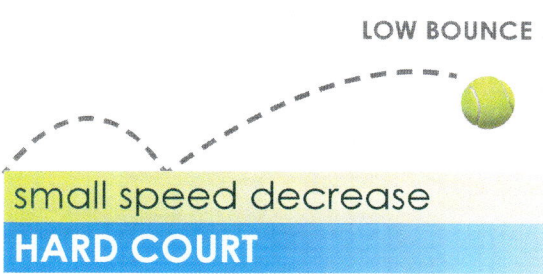

LOW BOUNCE

small speed decrease
HARD COURT

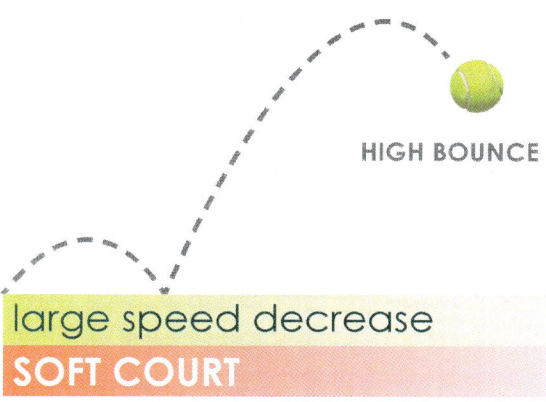

HIGH BOUNCE

large speed decrease
SOFT COURT

advanced practicing

advanced practicing

SERVING STROKE
PIN CRUSHER (PIN RULES)

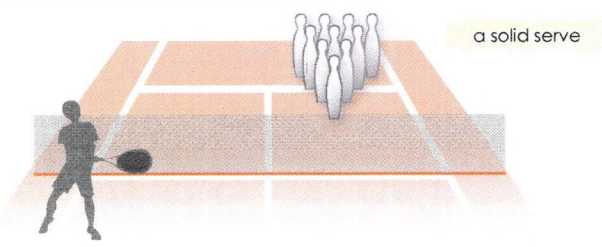

a solid serve

- position the pins on the court as you would play the real pinball but this time with the tennis ball
- apply the scoring from original game and gradually increase the score you'd like to reach, e.g. 30, 40...

BIN CRUSHER (1 OR 3)

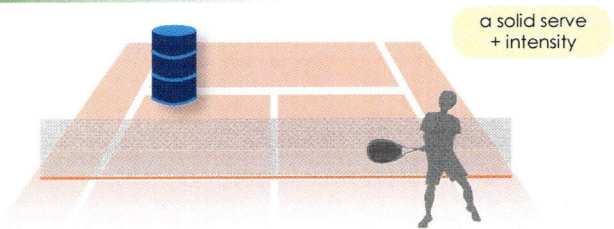

a solid serve
+ intensity

- place 1 big bin on the place where you want to place a serve and try to hit the target
- you can modify this practicing by increasing the number of used bins or by trying various objects

CONTROL PRACTICING
5-0 (COUNTDOWN)

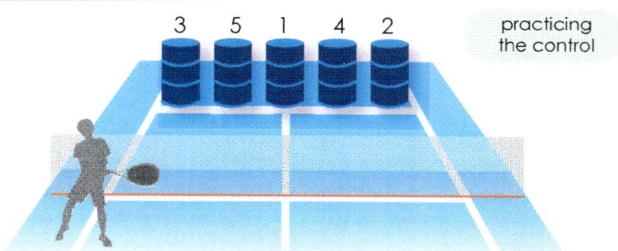

practicing the control

- mark 5 bins by numbers so you know which to hit
- hit the bins in ascending or descending order either from static (serving) position or by returning the balls launched by ball launcher or by you playing partner

COUNT TO X

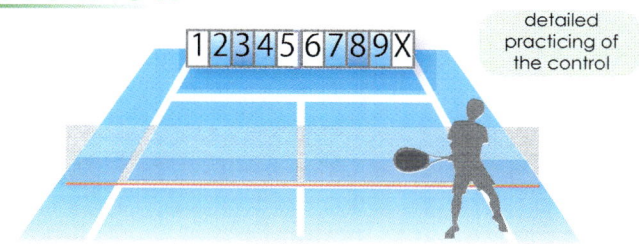

detailed practicing of the control

- place bins or any objects with numbers starting from 1 to 10 (X) so you can hit them in ascending or desc. order like you did in previous practice
- modify it, for example: hit the odd numbers only, etc.

advanced practicing

advanced practicing

PRACTICING THE SERVING STROKES

- if the rules allow always use **contrast sun glasses** to be able to lock the flying ball even in strong sunlight
- having powerful shots is very important when you are aiming to improve your game, however
  CONTROL ON THE COURT IS THE DECISIVE FACTOR
- control your **mind awareness on court at all times** with these simple **PRE-GAME & IN-GAME EXERCISES**:
    - practice **from less & bigger to more & smaller targets**
    - you need to train your mind to **be prepared for much challenging conditions** than is the practicing
    - first program yourself for hitting target from static position, then for hitting **any target in movement**
    - set yourself **smaller goals first**, then ask for more
    - "I have to hit 5 times in a row."
    - **DO NOT TOLERATE MISTAKES during practicing**, if you are not 100% effective, start all over again
    - it will take hours, days, weeks, months but you will **PLAY BETTER THAN THE REST** of the playing field
- learn to play your racket as good as it can get

PRACTICING VARIABLE STROKES

- use a similar strategy as with serving when **playing with ball launcher**
- it **can be modified** in multiple ways so you can utilize variable shots to make your ability to play become more flexible than ever before

MY RACKET SPECIFICATION

POWER ☆ ☆ ☆ ☆ ☆ ☆ ☆ ☆ ☆ ☆

ANGLE ☆ ☆ ☆ ☆ ☆ ☆ ☆ ☆ ☆ ☆

CONTROL ☆ ☆ ☆ ☆ ☆ ☆ ☆ ☆ ☆ ☆

STRINGING ☆ ☆ ☆ ☆ ☆ ☆ ☆ ☆ ☆ ☆

GRIP ☆ ☆ ☆ ☆ ☆ ☆ ☆ ☆ ☆ ☆

Is this a good racket for my actual game?   YES   NO

What would I like to improve with my actual racket?

_____

_____

How should my new racket differ from actual racket?

_____

_____

Personal notes and observations about my actual racket:

_____

_____

_____

_____

advanced practicing

advanced practicing

HORIZONTAL AIM (center with most points)

focusing on target

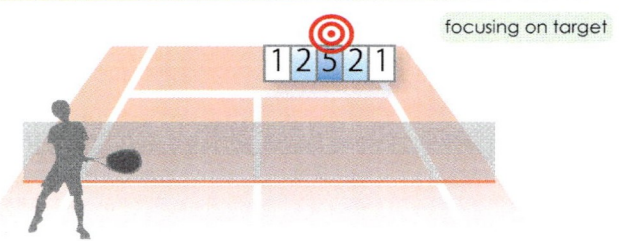

- the numbers on the boxes or bins represent the classic **bulls eye target (in this case in horizontal positioning)**
- the total width of the target area gives you initial freedom of learning to hit 1 large target
- make them **bigger or smaller**, reduce or increase the number of them for making this practice easier or challenging depending on your own expectations
- the goal is to gain basic feel for hitting one specific place on the court **without over-thinking it** in real match
- sommetimes it's good to use **affirmations**; create your own affirmations or use the one below

My playing opponent is a target - bin, number, box, bucket, whatever I am practicing with. My playing opponent is extremely versatile target. This target I either want to hit with the tennis ball or I want to avoid hitting it. He will be very responsive to my playing style and he will do whatever it takes to crush me. But I am dangerous as well because I do practice hard and smart for to be prepared for any challenge.

PRACTICE - EASY, ADVANCED, HARD

- practices help us to prepare for the real game
- **winners** do always practice and they practice regularly so when they enter the tournament arena they feel as comfortable as possible (no fear, no pressure)

- your own practices should be divided into **easy, advanced and professional levels**
- train wisely because as your body, your mind can be overloaded as well
- the past should be **your teacher** and not your enemy
- learn from the past victories or even mistakes but allow them to control you in positive way only **to become better by every new game, set or match**
- set yourself smaller goals first, then make them bigger
- you must feel relaxed, **take your time** for rehearsal & let your body calm down

> ALWAYS THINK ONLY ABOUT NEXT SHOT
> **BECAUSE YOU WILL NEVER HAVE OPPORTUNITY TO REPAIR A SHOT FROM THE PAST**

- in practicing you can use anything possible to help you correct your orientation to the target
- don't forget to practice with professional tennis coach on regular basis to make your progress consistent

advanced practicing

advanced practicing

SPELL TENNIS

variability

- for this practice use **bins or even buckets** with the letters of any preferable word, we chose to use the word TENNIS
- the bins or the buckets should have an open top without a lid so we can **utilize various types of shots**
- try to **hit the buckets with the ball** directly or the ball inside of them in an order in which the name TENNIS will be spelled correctly
- place the buckets in the **correct spelling order** in the beginning of this practice, later on, as the practice will continue, place them randomly so it will be a **more challenging** for you, e.g. turn around
- and let your buddy switch the positions of buckets try to **use different sizes or color of the buckets**
- the possibilities of this practices are limited only by your imagination but always do follow a **basic rule for practices** described in this pocket guide (read below)
- if you will miss hit the target in an incorrect order, **start all over again** because the real game won't give you second chances for repairing your mistakes

PRACTICE & CHALLENGE YOURSELF

- 66. practices are made for you to feel great when winning
ENJOY HITTING THE BALL & CHANGES WILL COME
- 67. correct and regular practicing is making you a tough competitor for your opponents
- 68. once your opponent will feel that you are a difficult to defeat you will gain the control over actual match

**PLAY ALL SHOTS ON THE PRACTICING COURT
AS IT WOULD BE ON THE TOURNAMENT COURT**

- play during practices virtually just in your head, you don't have to walk anywhere
- when you will win in a practice match **enjoy it as it would be a real tournament**
- get used to the winning feeling and become hungry to achieve winning as much as possible
- work hard with your tennis coach and results will come

MENTAL PREPARATION

YOU ARE THE RULER OF YOUR EFFORT

- if you feel that your playing partners are not challenging enough, play against two or find more advanced playing partners
- don't be hasty, **make yourself comfortable** and then your game will advance to a higher level
- not every match will be easy to win therefore give yourself a time reserve for easing up after an unwanted shot because in a **real game it will be tough**

advanced practicing

mental strategies

STRATEGIES FOR THE TENNIS GAME

HOW TO FOCUS ON SUCCESSFUL SETTING AND ACHIEVING PREDETERMINED GOALS

INTENSIVE PRACTICING

- focus your concentration on PRIMARY goals
- remember, that you don't have to think about them in your actual game
- **make a hierarchy of** these **goals** fitted for yourself
  * you can do it alone or with a tennis coach
- every **new goal** should be a little bit **higher** than your actual level of playing

EVERY GOAL SHOULD BE **SPECIFIC AND ACHIEVABLE**

- set a **certain a time to accomplishment** a specific number **of goals**
- **for achieving** every **goal**, give yourself a small **gift** - this will **motivate** you to want and do more

YOU CHOOSE THE PATH, YOU SHAPE THE RESULT

- on the following pages, you can find examples of how your list of goals will look like:

GLOBAL STRATEGY
FOR ACHIEVING A GOAL #1

Player **with no playing experience** (goals for one month)

- 10 or more practice sessions with a tennis coach
- play two 1 set matches with a tennis coach

Player - **less experienced level** (goals for one month)

- play first hack tournament
- play two 1 set matches
- **5 practice sessions** with tennis coach

Player - **beginner playing level** (goals for one month)

- play 2 or more local tournaments
- play two or more 2 set matches
- **5 practice sessions** with tennis coach
- play 2 matches with at least **1 winning set**
- **win** at least **1 friendly match**
- **win** at least **1 match in local competition**

mental strategies

mental strategies

GLOBAL STRATEGY
FOR ACHIEVING A GOAL #2

Player - **advanced playing level** (goals for one month)

- **qualify for** 1 or more **district tournaments**
- play two or more 3 set matches
- **5 practice sessions** with tennis coach
- **play** 3 or more matches with at least **2 winning sets**
- win at least **1 local tournament**
- win at least 1 match in **district competition**

Player - **pro playing level** (goals for one month)

- **qualify for national tournament**
- play two or more 3 set matches
- **5 practice sessions** with tennis coach
- **play** 3 or more matches with at least **2 winning sets**
- win at least **1 district tournament**
- win at least 1 match in **national competition**
- **qualify to semi-final** of national tournament

ACTIVE STRATEGY
FOR ACHIEVING A GOAL

- set FOR yourself an ultimate main goal – to qualify for national open tournament
- all tennis courts are designed to be played and won by player of any gender, nationality, social status
- you should be able to overcome your fears and doubts and reach the goals you did set for yourself
- you can start to play on local tournaments
- regular practicing with a professional tennis coach is a MUST on the way to improve your game
- professional tennis coach is a person who will show you not only the way to play better, he will detect and repair mistakes you making right now
- you must play a lot to **get to know your game and understand, what are for you, the most important goals in your** active **strategy**
- strategies for achieving a goal can help you organize steps for improving your game and not to think about unnecessary thoughts which may hurt your score
- don't forget to prepare on the first service of the first game because this moment can determine how you will proceed during the whole round
- don't wait until tomorrow,

YOUR MOMENT IS NOW

- explore examples of active strategy stages:

mental strategies

mental strategies

ACTIVE STRATEGY
FOR ACHIEVING A GOAL

To play the best shot, you don't need trophies or rankings to play a correct shot. All you need is a clear mind. When a king goes into battle, he never wears a crown.

When facing a shot, put down all trophies and other unnecessary thoughts. Stand barefoot with only one thought - **SIMPLE MOVEMENT** and you will perform a **PERFECT SHOT**.

 peRFect shot

 game

 set

 match

5 STAGES TO APPROACH A WIN

5th stage goal

- set yourself a **BIG goal**, to win a specific GRAND SLAM TOURNAMENT, name it, **make a picture in your mind** that you are receiving a trophy; make a special place for it, make sure that you see it every time you go practicing and every time you come back from a tournament;

LET IT REMIND YOU:

"I HAVEN'T REACHED IT YET!"

4th stage goal

- set a goal to win a **MATCH**; if you want to compare yourself with excellent tennis players, you need to **start winning matches**; once you'll achieve it, you can tell that you have set a new standard for your game - "THIS IS MY STANDARD. I CAN PLAY IT. I CAN PLAY IT REGULARLY."

mental strategies

 *mental strategies*

3rd stage goal

- when facing a court, set yourself a goal to **WIN A SET** on it; it is not that difficult, you know that you already did hit a perfect service and you have already played in several challenging tournaments, **"I CAN DO IT AGAIN, I CAN DO IT WITH A SMILE!"**

2nd stage goal

- when facing a new game, set yourself a goal to **WIN A GAME** with ease;
  "I KNOW MY BODY, I KNOW MY RACKET, I KNOW MY, POSIBILITIES, MY GRIP IS STRONG, MY MIND IS CLEAR!"

1st stage goal

- when facing a shot, FORGET ALL GOALS and don't think about any of them; all you need to do is go back to the fundamentals
  GRIP, STANCE, RHYTHM

IF YOU ARE THINKING IN THE MOST INTIMATE MOMENT ABOUT ANYTHING OTHER THAN YOUR RACKET AND THE BALL YOU ARE CHEATING YOURSELF ON YOUR GAME

THE MOST INTIMATE MOMENT OF THE GAME

the place for TROPHY is on the shelf,

the MATCH score will be in tomorrow's newspapers,

the SET score will be shown on the score board

but before I will win a GAME

first I must make a WINNING SHOT

 | MATCH | SET | **game** | shot

mental strategies

GAME PLAY ROUTINE

ADVANCED FORMS OF GAME PLAY ROUTINE

- the more you improve your playing level, the more you will try to avoid risky play because you know that
EVERY POINT IS PRECIOUS
- one of the key elements in progress in the mental game of tennis is to **allow yourself to be better**
- to be better means to accept actual **best performance as YOUR GAME**
- in moment you achieve your new best score so far, try to play it repeatedly as many times as possible
- next step to be a **better mental player** goes through acceptance - achievement of winning status is your own game,

YOUR NEW STATUS

- if you will try to divide your games into those which are played just for fun and games which are more important, understand that every playing encounter determines your **progress or regress** in the game
- be ready to **control your self-confidence** because it is possible that lack of self-confidence will try to convince you that a better score was just pure coincidence

- actively **REACT ON YOUR EXPECTATIONS**, needs and results as this will create your **GAME PLAY ROUTINE**
- when you are practicing, try to remember what practicing technique made you **play better in the last match**
- although tennis is called a game - in serious game (competition) **there are no friends, just opponents**, just rivals; when starting a new round, shake their hands with respect but let them know with your eye contact that **you are not giving any round up for free**
- watch your game, record your success **step by step**, put trophies even those small ones, on a shelf somewhere where you can see them everyday
- compare data of your game = they can give you a lot priceless information about yourself and about your mind
- **let your game be evaluated** but only with a player who is better than you - a professional tennis coach is the most appropriate person to do so
- the more you play this game, the more you are going to look at it as science:
    - the more you can identify
    - the more you can describe
    - the more you can control
        - what do you feel and how do you act

game play routine

47

game play routine

ICARUS* ACTIVITY APPROACH
BALANCE YOUR SWING / BALANCE YOUR CONFIDENCE

 OVER EXCEEDED EXPECTATIONS

TOP break down zone (thin line)

STRONG FOCUSING
on achieving predetermined goals

HEALTHY GAME CONFIDENCE

LOOKING FOR EXCUSES
blaming on external factors

BOTTOM break down zone

 NEGATIVITY, LACK OF CONFIDENCE

maintaining the average level of healthy game confidence can guarantee you steady results, constant strengthening of confidence can give you more opportunities of **WIN** - see the **3 pillars of success**

YOU FLY TOO HIGH - YOU'LL BURN
YOU FLY TOO LOW - YOU'LL DROWN

* from the classic Greek myth of Daedalus and Icarus

PRE-TOURNAMENT WARM UP

- **warming up** - before a competitive match (tournament) it is a important part of game play routine
- use the next examples or create your own warm up routine

PREPARE YOUR MIND AND BODY IN ADVANCE

- relax before entering the tennis court
- the best way to avoid making an unwanted shot in the serving shot is to **have time reserved** for stretching & warming up practice; e.g. +/- 30 minutes
- to learn how to stretch body muscles in the proper way always contact a licensed professional, otherwise you'll assume the risk probability of an injury
- always **start with less powerful shots** which require smaller tension to your muscles: e.g. 5 shots with 10% of your power, 5 x 25%, 5 x 50%, 10 x 10%, 10 x 25%, 10 x 50% etc.
- never hit the first practicing shot with the racket with more than 50% of your maximal power
- the goal of hitting not more than 50-75 shots in warm up - you want to renew/restart the muscle memory only
- you need to **warm up your muscles** & not getting tired
- you don't need to think about other player
- make sure to reserve a 10 minutes warm up for net game (volleying) - **as it can become a decisive factor in overall match score**
- try to find the **best balance and rhythm for yourself**

> **VICTORY IS ALWAYS A PRIORITY, BUT NEVER A GOAL, BECAUSE YOU CAN NEVER LOSE A TOURNAMENT, ONLY THE SHOT**

game play routine

game play routine

EACH GAME IS AN EXPERIMENT

- watch conditions under which **you are successful** & pretend to be a scientist, it's fun and it's useful
- if you will recognize, that is to say - **identify, describe and control** conditions of your success at one place, you willbe able to use them **anywhere you will need**
- if you don't know them yet - you will
- professional tennis coach should be able to help you to **find your game routine**
- the more data you gain (the more you play), the stronger results you will obtain - and re-use
- modify **possibilities and conditions** under which you play until you will be successful
- use every one of your practicing or tournament matches for comparing gathered data
- one of the most obvious reasons of not-winning is that tennis players play with rackets not-fitted for their game
- ask your professional tennis coach for these options
- another common issue is that players expect to be great in every aspect of the game - modern history of tennis shows us that there are players who were better servers, net players, better mental players, etc.

YOU MUST FIND WHAT YOU ARE BEST AT

ADJUSTING VARIABLES

IF YOU play a match and not loosing a game/set while playing a tournament with appropriate field of players (which will be a better result in continuity comparing to other friendly matches) **without stimuluses that are limiting your potential, eliminate or lower their influence!**

- if you play the best match of your life without music bumping through your headphones, DO NOT ever listen to it while practicing on the tennis court
- if you play the best match of your life without father who is pushing you to get better results every time DO NOT ever take him with you for practicing, nor for a tournament
- if you play the best match of your life without lucky charm, talisman, favorite cap, which was given to you as a birthday gift from your wife, LEAVE IT at home
- if you play the best match of your life without any unnecessary thoughts about the game performance, LET THEM GET OUT OF YOUR HEAD forever
- if you play the best match of your life without... any other THING which you did not ever need throw away everything what is preventing you to

Think & Play The Easy Way

game play routine

PRACTICE WITH PROFESSIONAL TENNIS COACH!

- after you **work hard enough** to get the results of this psychological experiment which you could be able to repeat, practice with professional tennis coach even more than you have practiced before
- knowledge of the stronger or the weaker aspects of your game will help you to tell the PRO more specific indications to the next step
- ONE VERY IMPORTANT THING - you must understand & accept that it's not likely to **reach 100% rate of success**
- take it easy next time and don't waste energy on blaming stupid rackets, balls, court, weather because maybe it's just not your day
- there are many variables and most of them are external; you have only **one STEADY POINT** – creating your own playing routine - **a gameplay corner stone**
- there is an immense need for you to practice with certified professional tennis coach
- IF YOU ARE NOT progressing with one tennis coach, switch to another
- maybe one day it will be **you** who will take home the **silverware replica**

SELF-CONFIDENCE

BELIEF
AS A PSYCHOLOGICAL FACTOR IN THE GAME

belief in yourself, belief in victory - 2 ways:

A conscious or non-conscious orienting on securing conditions which could **rise the possibility of a victory** as high as possible (professional guidance, healthy life style, time management etc.)

B belief that you can hold on to other forces other than your own - talismans, lucky charms, etc., **anything but not your own ability**

- these items are used as powerful and intensive self-motivating objects which reject negative thoughts and possible endings of a desired action
- belief, creed can be a fantastic & tremendous HELP, BUT it can destroy your **healthy self confidence** in the moment when you have given every bit of your investment to achieve specific goals
- in the moment of the use of external factors you may choose - to hold on either to something which is virtual or scientifically validated

self-confidence

self-confidence

REMINDER

The stressful situations arise from time to time. We start to feel pressured because we don't know how to continue. Our sub-consciousness pushes us to avoid this pressure so we make quick decisions. These decisions we wouldn't make under normal conditions. Here are some basic rules we should to follow.

The real Advantage

belongs to a player who focuses on actual shot rather than anything else which is not relevant to the presence because

VICTORY IS ALWAYS ACHIEVED ONE POINT AT A TIME

You need
A. **1 SHOT TO WIN A POINT**
B. **4 points** to win **a game**
C. **6 games** to win **a set**
D. **2 or 3 sets** to win **a match**

7 main areas to practice regularly

1. mental game
2. technical
3. cardio
4. running
5. strong arms / strong legs
6. strong core
7. stretching

	POWER	**FLEXIBILITY**	**PLAYER TYPE**
HEAVY HEAD	more	smaller	baseline
LIGHT HEAD	less	bigger	nett

YOU ARE THE ONE

- psychological pressure moments which are coming during play have no origin in quality towards your opponent or the unfair umpire and certainly not from non-functional lucky charms
- psychological pressure rises in your head with your thoughts, your initiative (mostly non-conscious) and

YOU ARE THE ONLY ONE WHO CAN CONTROL IT

self-confidence

self-confidence

MIND, POWER & CONTROL

- it is your mind that controls the power added to your arms during the shot (power by total vs. partial intensity)
- it is your hands that create rotation & path of the racket
- it is the racket that dictates the trajectory of the flight of the ball
- it is the landing point of the ball which creates the emotions - positive, neutral or negative
- practice a lot & practice with tennis PRO to find connection on the journey from mind control to desired emotion

identify, describe & control

To understand the natural path of the shot try to swing with weight on a string. Feel the motion that is created and transform it to your tennis shot. You'll soon find that you don't need to use lot of power to get more advantage.

MIND MUST BE BALANCED
RHYTHM MUST BE BALANCED
SHOT MUST BE BALANCED

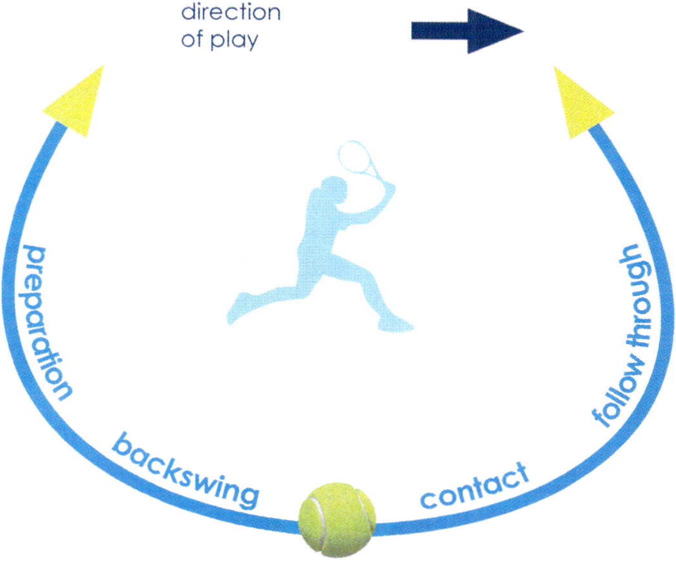

direction of play

preparation

backswing

contact

follow through

example **Monte-Carlo**
backswing and follow through - to remain the same time interval, use 2 easy to remember words of two syllables

self-confidence

mental game achievements

TROPHY CASE OF MENTAL ACHIEVEMENTS

- practice with tennis PRO, play, compete & get to the crown of all trophies
- enjoy your progress when checking the achievements

Win all ☐ trophies

1st WIN ☐ **national tournament**

1st match ☐ **WIN** national tournament

Qualify for ☐ national open tournament

1st WIN ☐ **of** district tournament

1st match ☐ **WIN** in district tournament

No set ☐ **lost** in match

2 consec. ☐ **friendly match wins**

1st win in ☐ friendly match

1st two ☐ winning sets

1st WIN ☐ set in 1 match

1st WIN ☐ game in 1 set

No Faults ☐ in the match

2 or less ☐ **faults** per match

5 or less ☐ **faults** per match

10 or less ☐ **faults** per match

My toughest opponents _____

3 YOUR MIND

What are **the 3 most precious thoughts** that you allow to enter into your mind in last seconds **before THE SHOT?**

Write down the most common thoughts you have when you're facing the shot. Reduce them 3 times so at the end you'll have just 3 most important of them. This will make your choice easier when facing real challenge.

You need no more than 3 thoughts in critical situation. FREE YOUR MIND!

free your mind

scorechart

SCORECHART #1

Detailed score from 10 matches

Match No.	RES W/L	sets won	sets lost	0's	15's	30's	40's	games won	games lost	tie break	faults

Keep tracking your match scores in details. RES W/L - result W for match won, result L for match that was lost

RECORD, INTERNALIZE & PROGRESS!

SCORECHART #2

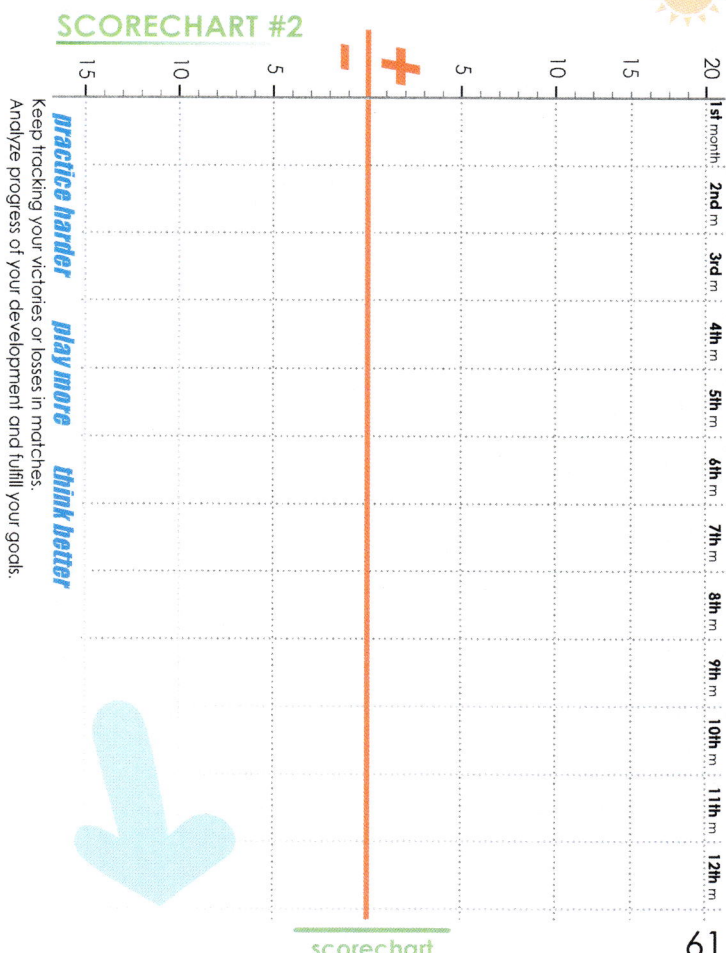

practice harder   play more   think better

Keep tracking your victories or losses in matches.
Analyze progress of your development and fulfill your goals.

scorechart

 **in the bag** checklist

IN THE BAG CHECK LIST

CONTROL YOUR "IN THE BAG CHECKLIST" IN ADVANCE!

Practicing BAG
- primary set of rackets (in pairs)
- secondary set of rackets
- water/sport drink
- food
- towel
- extra clothes (hat, wristbands, etc.)
- grips
- practicing aids (balls, etc.)

Competition BAG
MIN. 2 RACKETS IN THE BAG
- set of rackets (in pairs - 2,4,6, etc.) ◯
- water ◯
- food ◯
- towel ◯
- extra grips ◯
- t-shirts ◯ pants ◯ shoes ◯
- accessories ◯
- tape ◯ string dampeners ◯ sunglasses ◯
- special equipment ◯
- membership card / pro card ◯

MY TENNIS GOALS

- write down your tennis goals for a year in advance
- goal should be specific & achievable
- set a certain a time to accomplishment every goal on the list
- for accomplishing every goal, give yourself a small gift

I choose the path & I determine the results!

goal	date
goal	date
goal	date
goal	date
goal	date
goal	date
goal	date
goal	date
goal	date
goal	date

tennis goals

CUSTOM GLOBAL STRATEGY FOR ACHIEVING A GOAL #1

Player **with no playing experience** (goals for one month)

STAGE 1 - achieved in ___ month/s ◯

◯ ___ or more practice sessions with a tennis coach
◯ play ___ 1 set matches with PRO tennis coach

Player - **less experienced level** (goals for one month)

STAGE 2 - achieved in ___ month/s ◯

◯ play first hack tournament
◯ play ___ 1 set matches
◯ ___ practice sessions with PRO tennis coach

Player - **beginner playing level** (goals for one month)

STAGE 3 - achieved in ___ month/s ◯

◯ play ___ local tournaments
◯ play two or more 2 set matches
◯ ___ practice sessions with PRO tennis coach
◯ play 2 matches with at least ___ winning set
◯ win at least ___ friendly match
◯ win at least ___ match in local competition

CUSTOM GLOBAL STRATEGY
FOR ACHIEVING A GOAL #2

Player - **advanced playing level** (goals for one month)

STAGE 4 - achieved in ___ month/s ⬜

- ⬜ qualify for ___ or more district tournaments
- ⬜ play two or more 3 set matches
- ⬜ ___ or more practice sessions with tennis coach
- ⬜ play 2 matches with at least ___ winning sets
- ⬜ win at least ___ local tournament
- ⬜ win at least ___ match in district tournament

Player - **higher playing level** (goals for one month)

STAGE 5 - achieved in ___ month/s ⬜

- ⬜ qualify for national tournament
- ⬜ play two or more 3 set matches
- ⬜ ___ or more practice sessions with tennis coach
- ⬜ play 2 matches with at least ___ winning sets
- ⬜ win at least ___ district tournament
- ⬜ win at least ___ match in national tournament
- ⬜ qualify to semi-final of national tournament

custom global strategies

practicing plan

PRACTICING PLAN A

- write down your practice plan, it will help you set your direction

date	power
	control
date	power
	control
date	power
	control
date	power
	control
date	power
	control
date	power
	control
date	power
	control
date	power
	control

PRACTICING PLAN B

- write down your practice plan, it will help you set your direction

date	power
	control
date	power
	control
date	power
	control
date	power
	control
date	power
	control
date	power
	control
date	power
	control
date	power
	control

virtual pressure serve

VIRTUAL PRESSURE - SERVICE PRACTICE 1

Virtual practice helps to create a status similar to a real game. Record your serving status and face the challenging conditions in this practicing so that you can feel more relaxed and comfortable in the real match.

PRACTICING IS EASY, THE REAL GAME IS TOUGH

RULES
Virtualize, imagine in your mind that

THERE'S NO ROOM FOR ERRORS

1. You can't make any faults. If you will make a fault in the service, you will fail. The Goal is to have most **flawless serves** combined with most of the **gains**.
2. The big number is *a number of your serve*. Under the **srvc** write the number of services you did need until you served correctly. Note that some beginners do need more attempts in the practicing.
3. Under the **gain** check the check box - **if you were able to make a correct service at 1st time** or leave it empty - **if you serviced more than once - with 1 or more faults**.
4. **Gains** refer to cumulative number of services on 1 attempt you made in 1 game. Why only 4 serving boxes?
5. **If you need more than 4 services in 1 game, you lost**. This practice is difficult but it will make you a tough competitor.
6. The **result** will tell if you won or lost this tough challenge.

example

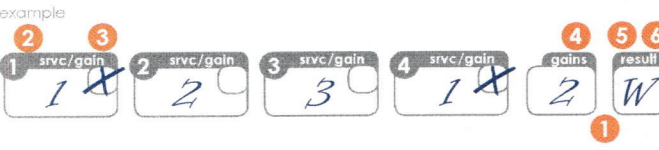

VIRTUAL PRESSURE SERVE PRACTICE 2

virtual pressure serve

list of mistakes

LIST OF MISTAKES

Record mistakes you make during the game so you don't forget them. Return to them after and work hard on correcting them. **Repair & never repeat!**

fixed

fixed

Pick the toughest ones which made you practice harder & play better after the correction

PRACTICE WITH TENNIS PRO - CALENDAR

_____ issue/name of the tennis PRO _____ date ◯

_____ issue/name of the tennis PRO _____ date ◯

_____ issue/name of the tennis PRO _____ date ◯

_____ issue/name of the tennis PRO _____ date ◯

_____ issue/name of the tennis PRO _____ date ◯

_____ issue/name of the tennis PRO _____ date ◯

_____ issue/name of the tennis PRO _____ date ◯

_____ issue/name of the tennis PRO _____ date ◯

_____ issue/name of the tennis PRO _____ date ◯

_____ issue/name of the tennis PRO _____ date ◯

_____ issue/name of the tennis PRO _____ date ◯

_____ issue/name of the tennis PRO _____ date ◯

- this Practice with a tennis PRO calendar will help you to watch your practicing routine and issues you're working on in a time table
- you need to fill this calendar fully with hand signature of certified tennis teaching professional

practice with PRO calendar

evaluation

EVALUATION

- from last competitive matches write down:
  1. what made you feel good
  2. what made you feel poorly
- compare both evaluations & mark the one which exceeds + or -

CUSTOM ACTIVE STRATEGY - THE GOAL OF ALL GOALS

1 _____

2 _____

3 _____

4 _____

5 _____

Create your own Active strategy for achieving your ultimate goal. Rethink, analyze and calculate all possibilities that should lead you to your ultimate goal.

May you achieve your Goals & Dreams!

custom active strategy

rankngs

MY POSITIONS IN THE TOURNAMENTS

Nr. position   score   date   name of the tournament/opponent

1.
2.
3.
4.
5.
6.
7.
8.
9.
10.
11.
12.
13.
14.
15.

Learn the easy way.

Learn "How to learn" in the easiest and the most efficient way.

Adjust your learning experience to your age, abilities and expectations.

For students who want to save their grades, as well as for students who want nothing but the best results at all levels, all the time.

court map indicators

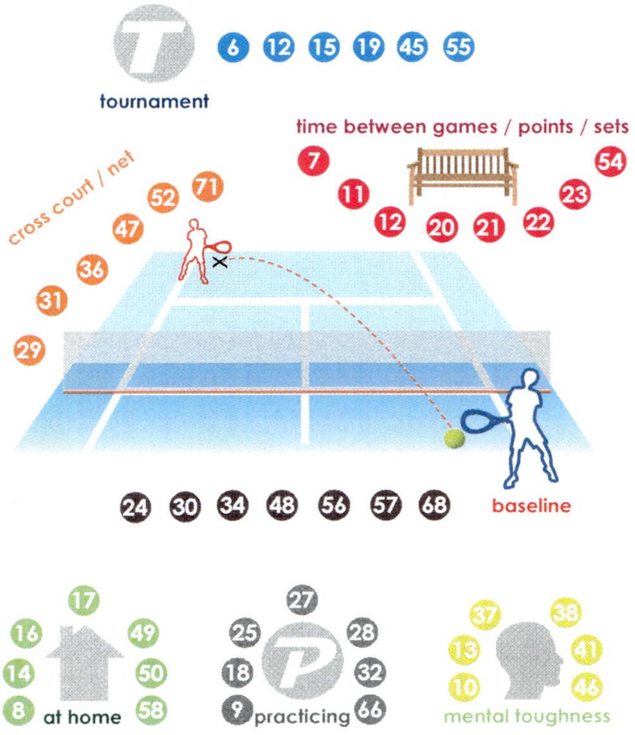

COURT MAP INDICATORS

tournament — 6, 12, 15, 19, 45, 55

cross court / net — 29, 31, 36, 47, 52, 71

time between games / points / sets — 7, 11, 12, 20, 21, 22, 23, 54

baseline — 24, 30, 34, 48, 56, 57, 68

at home — 8, 14, 16, 17, 49, 50, 58

practicing — 9, 18, 25, 27, 28, 32, 66

mental toughness — 10, 13, 37, 38, 41, 46

The court map indicators is the visual system of integrated hints on which pages in this book you can quickly find info related to the main topic e.g. playing situation from base line.

INDEX OF KEY PHRASES

ABILITY - 9, 12, 45, 66, 68, 70, 72

ACHIEVING - 45, 58, 63, 64, 66, 68, 71, 72

APPROACH - 48, 56, 64, 68, 71

BEFORE THE GAME - 49, 59, 62, 63, 70, 71

CONFIDENCE - 58, 63, 68, 71, 72

CONTROL - 33, 45, 53, 54, 56, 60, 68, 71

COURT MANAGEMENT - 56, 66, 68, 71, 72

DOMINATION - 33, 54, 56, 68, 71

EMOTIONS - 6, 7, 8, 9, 11, 12, 14, 27, 51, 53, 55, 56, 59

IMMEDIATE RESPONSE - 6, 7, 18, 19, 20, 22, 27

IN DA GAME - 7, 12, 13, 14, 15, 20, 22

MENTAL STRENGTH - 15, 63, 64, 66, 68, 71, 72

MOTIVATION - 6, 63, 64, 66, 70, 71

ON VICTORY FOCUSED - 6, 33, 45, 56, 62

POWER - 45, 53, 66, 68, 71

PRACTICING - 28, 29, 30, 31, 34, 35, 36, 37, 52, 66, 68, 71, 72

PRE - TOURNAMENT - 49, 62, 63, 64, 68, 71, 72

PREPARATION - 62, 64, 68, 70, 71, 72

PRESSURE - 6, 20, 22, 59, 68, 70, 71

RE - THINKING - 53, 54, 56, 63, 66, 68, 70, 71, 72

REASONING - 11, 14, 15, 56, 63, 71, 72

RELAXING - 6, 16, 17, 19, 20, 21

RHYTHM - 54, 56, 57, 71

SCIENCE - 8, 9, 28, 29, 30, 31, 33, 50, 51, 61, 72

STRATEGY - 38, 39, 40, 41, 42, 43, 44, 56, 63, 64, 68, 71, 72

STRESS - 8, 9, 42, 45, 48, 54, 55, 59, 67, 71, 72

TRAJECTORY - 33, 54, 57, 58, 68, 71

UNWANTED / UNEXPECTED SHOT - 6, 7, 20, 22, 68, 71

VICTORY - 6, 45, 53, 56, 60, 64, 68, 71

key phrases

MAIN THEMES

WELCOME
HOW TO USE IT — 4
PLAY BETTER — 6
IMMEDIATE RESPONSE — 7
PSYCHOLOGY & TENNIS — 8
Pressure & performance 8 | Psychology - mental advantage 9
TENNIS & STRESS — 10
Origin of stress 10 | Situation, reaction, reasoning 11 | Reverse process of stress 12 | Time & other issues management 13 | Clearing the visualization 14 | The most important shot 15
RELAXING TECHNIQUES — 16
Relaxing before practicing 17 | Tunnel of attention 18 | Relaxing before the game/shot 19 | Relaxing after the shot 22
RETHINKING OF MENTAL APPROACH — 22
The Rule of trivial domination 22 | Rethinking 23
COGNITIONS & TENNIS — 24
Three pillars of success 26 | Clear vision 27
ADVANCED PRACTICING TECHNIQUES — 28
Playing conditions 29 | Pin/bin crusher 30 | 5-0/Count to X 31 | Service 32 | My racket 33 | Horizont 34 | Spell 36 | Pre-game 37
MENTAL STRATEGIES — 38
Focusing on achieving predetermined goal 38 | Global strategy 39 | Active strategy 41 | 5 stages to approach a win 43 | The most intimate moment of the game 45
GAME PLAY ROUTINE — 46
Icarus activity approach 48 | Pre-tournament warm-up 49 | Game is an experiment 50 | Adjusting variables 51 | Practice with tennis professional 52
SELF-CONFIDENCE — 53
Belief, creed as a psychological factor 53 | Reminder 54 | You are the one 55 | Mind, Power & Control 56 | Balance 57
TROPHY CASE OF MENTAL ACHIEVEMENTS — 58